Original title:
Planting Poetic Seeds

Copyright © 2025 Creative Arts Management OÜ
All rights reserved.

Author: Ophelia Ravenscroft
ISBN HARDBACK: 978-1-80567-027-8
ISBN PAPERBACK: 978-1-80567-107-7

Green Verses

In a garden of words, seeds take their flight,
A haiku grows tall, then shivers with fright.
The daisies do giggle, the roses do tease,
While the tulips complain, 'Oh, give us some cheese!'

Squirrels in bow ties, writing sonnets at dawn,
Chasing after acorns, till their tails are drawn.
The worms wear top hats in their underground dance,
While the daisies debate, 'Should we take a chance?'

Blooming via the Pen

Once I wrote poems that sprouted and bloomed,
But my pen was a shovel, oh boy, I was doomed!
I dug all my rhymes like potatoes in dirt,
Now I harvest bad puns, and they really hurt!

My inkpot's a garden, it grows with a laugh,
My metaphors sprout, like a whimsical calf.
When the sun shines bright, and the wordplay's in bloom,
We dance around stanzas, avoiding the gloom!

Rhythms of the Harvest

In the field of odd rhymes, we sow what we sing,
A chorus of crickets, oh, what joy they bring!
With crows as my chorus, I harvest the sun,
And giggle at carrots that think they're more fun!

The stalks sway and shuffle, they tap and they groove,
While I pluck all the lines, in a funky move.
Bees buzzing along, keep the beat oh so right,
It's a symphony of nonsense, from morning to night!

Roots in the Rhyme

My roots twist and tangle, like verses gone wild,
Each line is a sprout, oh, so poorly styled.
The grass tickles toes, in a giggly spree,
Where dandelions rhyme with a very loud 'wee!'

In a patch of good humor, I kick up my heels,
As the veggies debate all their fanciest meals.
Lettuce whispers secrets, while potatoes just smile,
Creating a garden that's quirky in style!

The Color of Words

In the garden of my mind, words bloom,
They sprout like daisies, chasing off gloom.
With a sprinkle of laughter, and a dash of rhyme,
Each line grows taller, defying time.

Like rainbow-colored veggies, they dance and sway,
Tickling the senses, in a playful ballet.
Sometimes they trip, and tumble about,
But their silly antics are what it's about.

Evergreen Enchantments

In a forest of puns, where the tall trees giggle,
Every whisper of wind makes the branches wiggle.
Leaves of sarcasm rustle high in the air,
While roots of laughter tickle, beyond compare.

Mossy tales sprout like green spaghetti,
With each twist and turn, they keep it ready.
Nature's comedy show, an endless spree,
Where jokes bloom freely, just wait and see!

The Pollen of Ideas

Buzzing thoughts like bees, they flit and fly,
Sipping sweet nectar from the mind's pie.
A sprinkle of giggles, a dash of cheer,
Ideas flutter in, with a wink and a leer.

They land on pages, all funny and bright,
Creating a garden of laughter and light.
Each pollen grain spitting out a new tale,
Making us chuckle, we'd never pale!

Tapestries of Growth

Woven threads of humor in a tapestry grand,
Colors of joy made by our own hand.
With stitches of wit seamed close together,
Making patterns of laughter, light as a feather.

Now watch as they grow, like grass in the sun,
Each line a giggle, each verse a pun.
In the fields of our minds, we harvest delight,
Unraveling joy, turning wrongs into right.

Tending to Thoughts

In the garden of my mind,
Thoughts dance like weeds, unconfined.
I water them with coffee spills,
And jokes that grow like daffodils.

The dreams are sprouting, quite absurd,
Like rabbits hopping, have you heard?
With every laugh, a new seed's sown,
In this crazy field I've grown.

Sunshine helps my humor bloom,
While shadows chase away the gloom.
Digging deep with a shovel of glee,
I cultivate my mind's debris.

When silly thoughts begin to sprout,
I know there's joy, without a doubt.
With snickers and giggles, I tend my plot,
In this wild garden, I've got a lot!

A Symphony of Stems

In orchards rich with puns and plays,
The stems conduct in funny ways.
Each blossom bursts with laughter's cheer,
A symphony that we hold dear.

The daisies dance in happy twirls,
While tulips wiggle, making swirls.
Each stem's a note, each petal, a rhyme,
Growing in rhythm, keeping time.

Grasshoppers join with chirps that sing,
They take the stage, a lively fling.
With every hop and joyful jive,
They animate this giggling hive.

So gather 'round, let laughter sprout,
In this garden, there's never doubt.
Together we'll sing with hearts aglow,
In nature's symphony, let's take a bow!

Flourishing Imagery

In the canvas of the land so bright,
Imagery blooms, a comical sight.
With colors bright and strokes so bold,
Each quirky thought is ready to unfold.

A clown-shaped tree, so oddly tall,
Juggling fruits, it has a ball.
Breezes carry whispers of jest,
In this vibrant grove, we're all blessed.

Imagined critters waddle by,
With floppy ears and sparkling eye.
Each laugh a seed that bursts with zest,
In this wild world, we are impressed.

Creating visions from cheeky dreams,
Giggling rivers flow like streams.
This garden flourishes, full of cheer,
Where funny faces bloom year by year!

Nature's Lullaby of Words

A lullaby sung by blooming trees,
With crickets playing tunes on the breeze.
Each word takes flight like a cheeky bird,
In this chorus, laughter is stirred.

The leaves rustle with giggles and spins,
As daisies whisper sweet little sins.
In this patch of joy, the bugs take part,
Every chirp is a masterpiece of art.

The moon winks down on playful nights,
Sprinkling dreams with silly sights.
In a dandelion's wish, I can find,
A garden of humor, one of a kind.

So close your eyes and drift away,
Let nature's lullaby guide your play.
In the melody of joy's embrace,
Find a moment of humor and grace!

From Silt to Sonnet

In the garden of rhymes, I dig with glee,
A trowel of laughter, come dance with me.
Earthworms tap-dance, they wiggle and squirm,
Whispering secrets that wiggle and affirm.

With each turn of soil, ideas sprout wide,
Bumblebees buzzing, they won't let them hide.
Spreading the pollen of playful delight,
In this patch of nonsense, our dreams take flight.

Growth Rings of Expression

Like trees we venture, with wisdom spread thin,
Counting the rings where the giggles begin.
Each bark of a joke, a layer of fun,
In the forest of puns, we all become one.

Saplings of laughter, they reach to the sun,
Shade from the sappiness, oh what a run!
Branches of stories twist with a sigh,
As we reach for the sky, we're all butterflies.

Weaving Words with Nature

A tapestry woven with splashes of cheer,
Nature's own humor is bright and sincere.
The daisies giggle, their petals a-flutter,
While dandelions prank with a fluffy putter.

As spiders spin webs, they prattle away,
Spinning tall tales of their grand masquerade.
Each thread is a pun, a twist of delight,
In this garden of whimsy, our heart takes flight.

Harvest Moon Reflections

Under the moon, we gather, we cheer,
With pumpkins abounding, there's nothing to fear.
The stars wink in laughter, shining so bright,
As we scurry for apples in the cool of the night.

Chattering with critters, they join in our fun,
Raccoons tell tales of their sneaky run.
With a slap on the back and a dance on the green,
We toast to the harvest, the silliest scene.

Nectar of New Beginnings

In a garden where giggles grow,
I trip over weeds, oh no, oh no!
A bee steals my hat, buzzing away,
Why'd I come here? I should just play!

With boots covered in dirt, I dive,
A dance with the earth, I feel alive.
A worm appears, doing the twist,
Did I just see that? I can't resist!

I sprinkle some jokes along the way,
Watch laughter bloom at the end of the day.
A flower with socks? How rare, I cheer!
Blossoms of chuckles, nature's souvenir!

So here's to the fun as we sow and grow,
Let's giggle and wiggle, let the good times flow!
With nectar of humor, we start anew,
In this garden of joy, there's space for you!

Echoes in the Soil

Digging deep, I hear a call,
Is that a potato teasing, after all?
With carrots gossiping about the sun,
I laugh so hard, my work is done!

A cabbage rolls, trying to be bold,
"Tell me a secret!" it says, or so I'm told.
A radish with jokes makes the soil quirk,
Who knew roots had such comedic work?

I toss in some rhymes with a shimmy and shake,
As daisies dance, a more funny scene to make.
In this patch of giggles, we grow and shout,
Echoes of laughter are what it's about!

So come join the fun, let's dig and explore,
With laughs in the air, let's always want more!
In the soil of our humor, let it be bright,
Together, we're growing in goofy delight!

Flourish of the Written Word

Writers gather, planting their quips,
With ink-stained fingers, and funny scripts!
A pencil slips, oh what a scene,
As a story tumbles down like confetti green!

Words sprout up, giggling away,
In the garden of prose, they love to play.
An adjective winks, a noun strikes a pose,
Here, every tale tickles and glows!

Each sentence begins to bounce and sway,
Like rabbits in rhythm, hip-hip-hooray!
A plot twist flops, landing on its face,
But laughter nourishes this wild word space!

So let's pen parodies, jokes, and cheer,
With every scribble, the fun draws near.
In this flourish of laughter, let's make our mark,
A tapestry of joy, vibrant and stark!

Seeds of Thought Unfurled

A seed of humor, dropped with care,
Grows into giggles that dance in the air.
With sunshine bright, and laughter rained,\nA patch of funny vibes is what we've gained!

We sow our dreams, quirky and wild,
Like a child with candy, oh so beguiled.
Thoughts sprout wings, taking silly flight,
In this enchanted garden, everything feels right!

The roots of our laughter twist and twirl,
In the underground, they do a swirl.
Branches of joy reach up to the sky,
As leaves of laughter float drifting by!

So gather 'round, let's share our delight,
With seeds of joy, we'll keep it bright.
Here's to all minds, under sunshine unfurled,\nTogether we thrive in our giggly world!

Garden of Enigmas

In a garden where socks start to sprout,
Mysterious blooms that dance and shout.
Giggling tulips, with hats made of cheese,
Chasing the bees, oh what a tease!

Garden gnomes plotting, with eyes all aglow,
They trade whispers for seeds, oh where will they go?
A pumpkin once told me it was a car,
It drove off to Vegas—now it's a star!

Dandelions don capes, ready to fly,
While broccoli wonders how to say hi.
A parsnip in glasses reads books upside down,
In this quirky patch, there's never a frown!

So come join the chaos, the laughter, the jest,
In this wild plot, we're all just a guest.
Where celery dreams of being a fry,
And carrots invent how to bubble and fly!

Fertilizing Futures

In soil so rich, thoughts start to grow,
With eggshells and coffee, we start the show.
A hedgehog in coveralls, measuring the rain,
Says, 'I'll teach the sprouts how to dance in the lane!'

Fridge magnets whisper what seeds to sow,
Sardines on bicycles, oh what a flow!
The cabbages gossip about silly old trends,
While radishes bicker like long-lost friends.

A hoe sings a tune as it digs with delight,
And worms throw a party all through the night.
They argue and giggle about who's the best,
While soil takes notes for the next wild fest!

So toss in a joke while you nurture your plot,
Even zucchini can laugh—believe it or not!
Each sprout has a secret, a funny small tale,
In this garden of futures, where humor prevails!

Petals of Possibility

Petals with dreams of becoming a pie,
Twirl in the breeze, oh my to the sky!
The daisies declare it's a hat-making day,
And violets offer to sew on the sway.

A sunflower claims it's the next big star,
With petals that twinkle, it won't go too far.
The thyme insists on being the lead,
In this garden of whimsy, where all hearts can lead.

Why did the herb join a talent show spree?
It sang all the hits, from A to Z!
With mint in a pop-up and basil on drums,
Together they turned the garden to hums.

So dance with the petals and sway with the breeze,
In this wild, wild garden, do as you please!
For laughter is fertile, the fun never rots,
In this patch of all wonders, we'll give it some shots!

Tendrils of Creativity

Wiggly vines climb walls that are near,
With ideas that sprout, nothing to fear.
Beans wear top hats and strut their stuff,
While turnips recite poems, oh isn't that tough?

The kale likes to draw with a crayon for leaves,
While trivia spaceworms weave tales of thieves.
Spinach is crafting a masterpiece way,
Made of dreams, giggles, and a sprinkle of hay.

In this patch of tales and whimsical dreams,
The lettuce remembers where laughter redeems.
The carrots debate on who spins the best yarn,
With every odd story, the seeds become charm.

So wiggle your fingers and untie your hair,
In this world of odd thoughts, feel free if you dare!
For tendrils of joy wrap around in a twist,
In the garden of quirky, no fun can be missed!

Echoing Melodies of Meadow Minstrels

In the meadow, frogs sing loud,
A chorus, bold, draws quite the crowd.
Grasshoppers dance with merry glee,
Their tunes make even the daisies flee!

Bumblebees buzz a bumpy beat,
While daisies sway on tiny feet.
The wind joins in, a gusty friend,
Together they hum, on joy they depend!

Threads of Life Woven in Green

The vines are tangled, a playful mess,
Caterpillars claim them, no need to stress.
Each leaf a tale, a story spun,
Of ants on parade and mischief begun.

Rabbits hop by, in search of a snack,
Unruly greens, oh what a hack!
Nature's laughter, it bounces around,
In this leafy realm, pure joy can be found.

Beyond the Fence, a World of Words

A curious cat peers beyond the wood,
Whispers of wonders, oh how they should!
Chirping crickets share tales of night,
While fireflies twinkle—a dazzling sight!

Squirrels swap gossip, dart here and there,
With acorn debates that fill the air.
The fence may divide, yet laughter will soar,
Through gaps in the slats, we long to explore!

The Sustenance of Time's Garden

In the garden, time takes its bite,
Potatoes giggle, so round and bright.
Tomatoes blush like they're in a race,
With cucumbers flaunting their cool, green grace!

Carrots hide deep, they're shy little things,
While onions shed layers, oh what a sting!
The radishes chatter, quite bold and loud,
In this veggie realm, joy grows unbowed!

Whispers of the Growing Earth

In my garden, gnomes dance around,
Telling tales to worms underground.
They argue over who's the best sprout,
While I just nod, trying not to pout.

The daisies giggle as bees pass by,
While butterflies wear hats that are sky-high.
The carrots are plotting a secret bash,
While I await a salad; oh, what a clash!

A scarecrow knocked over his drink last night,
Now he's swaying like he's lost the fight.
The tomatoes are blushing, oh what a sight,
While radishes giggle at their weird plight.

So here's to the laughter among the blooms,
Where nature's nonsense surely resumes.
With every seed, a joke takes root,
In this quirky patch where silliness grew.

Verses in the Verdant Soil

In my backyard, a wild thing grew,
A cabbage with dreams, who always knew.
He wrote poetry while hard at work,
And gave the snails a good laugh with a quirk.

Sunflowers making plans for a play,
They called in the bugs, who came right away.
Crickets on strings, they strummed late at night,
While the toads croaked out choruses—what a sight!

The pumpkins, they jest about who is round,
While zucchini hides, feeling quite profound.
"Why so serious?" the peppers did say,
"Life is too short for a mundane day!"

So here we are, in this garden so bright,
Where laughter and joy bloom day and night.
With every giggle, the roots intertwine,
In this charming silliness, we truly shine.

Echoes of the Enchanted Grove

Underneath the oak, a squirrel's a bard,
Telling jokes that are simply quite hard.
He tickles the leaves as they rustle and sway,
"Why don't trees ever play hide and seek?" they say!

The mushrooms are giggling, all in a row,
Trading punchlines with the wind's gentle blow.
A fox cracks a grin, with a smirk so sly,
As the ferns sway in laughter, oh my, oh my!

The stream joins in with a bubbly laugh,
While wildflowers bloom, each one a staff.
They play sweet notes like a wacky song,
Inviting the critters to sing along.

So let's raise a cheer to the fun-loving green,
In this magical space, where silliness reigns supreme.
With every chuckle that dances in air,
The echoes ignite joy everywhere!

Blossoms of Barefoot Musings

Barefoot I roam through fields of gold,
Where daisies tell secrets that never get old.
With twinkling eyes, I watch them play,
As butterflies squeeze lemon juice all day!

The daisies spread gossip about the tall grass,
While the cacti complain that they don't have class.
"Why fit in?" chirps a bold little bloom,
"Let's cover this place with joy and some boom!"

A ladybug sports a tiny bow tie,
As she waltzes by with a curious sigh.
"Join my party!" she squeaks, full of flair,
While ants march on, without a care.

So here in the garden, with each little muse,
Every bloom shows us how to amuse.
Let's frolic and giggle and let spirits soar,
In this funny little world, who could ask for more?

Tilling the Terrain of Thought

With a shovel of giggles, I dig through my mind,
Uncovering treasures that are one of a kind.
Each thought is a sprout, with potential to grow,
Sometimes a weed, but hey, what do I know?

Moist laughter of memories, tilling the ground,
In the garden of quirkiness, joy can be found.
I dance with the daisies, I rhyme with the bees,
Who knew thoughts could tickle and sway in the breeze?

Rolling in laughter, as I cultivate dreams,
Mixing up humor with all of my schemes.
A hoe full of puns, a rake made of glee,
Tilling my terrain, I'm as happy as can be!

So let's plant some chuckles, let's sow lots of fun,
In this silly ol' garden, we each are the sun.
With laughter as soil, and joy as the rain,
My fertile imagination will never feel pain.

Sowing Stories

With a sprinkle of nonsense, I toss out my tales,
Each story a fish, to be caught by the gales.
I'm casting my lines with a wink and a cheer,
For the harvest of laughter will soon be right here!

A patch of wild fables, where giggles are grown,
Comedic crops flourish in soil unknown.
Each line a seedling, just waiting to sprout,
Watch it bloom into chaos—who knows what it's about?

These crops of silliness sway with the breeze,
Tickling the senses, like endless tickle trees.
Sowing again, with a grin full of wit,
My garden of stories, where laughter will fit!

So grab a good shovel and dig up some fun,
In this field of absurdity, we're never outdone.
May the stories we share, like wildflowers, grow,
And burst into laughter—oh, what a show!

Fertile Words

In the land of my thoughts, where ideas take root,
Each word is a whimsy, a curious fruit.
Nurtured with humor, grown over time,
These fertile words jive, in rhythm and rhyme.

Watch out for the puns—they can multiply fast!
A garden of giggles, where mischief is cast.
With every new phrase, I till up the soil,
From seed to bouquet, it all feels like toil!

These fertile words dance like weeds in the sun,
Some sprout like a cactus, others like fun.
In a plot full of laughter, we'll plant our mischief,
Growing lines without limits—no need for a sieve!

So let's reap what we sow, let's harvest our cheer,
In a world full of banter, let's lend an ear.
With every fresh phrase, a new bloom we'll find,
Fertile words of hilarity, lingering in kind.

The Tender Sprout

From a speck of an idea, a tender sprout peeks,
Wiggling and giggling, it wiggles its cheeks.
With the sun as its buddy, it stretches so wide,
Growing quirks in its petals, with joy as its guide.

Each leaf tells a story, sprout giggles galore,
Bouncing with laughter, it begs to explore.
Along came a breeze, with tickles and sighs,
This sprout's full of jest, a comedian in disguise!

The roots twist and tangle like jokes from the past,
While it reaches for humor that's meant to last.
A garden of whimsy, with grins and delight,
This tender sprout thrives, both day and night.

As it blossoms with joy, we can't help but cheer,
For each juicy chuckle, we secretly revere.
So here's to the sprout, that makes laughter abound,
In the heart of our garden, where joy can be found.

Dreams on the Wind

In my garden of dreams, I tossed a few wishes,
But the weeds grew taller, with humorous dishes.
The carrots cracked jokes as they sprouted so bright,
While the pumpkins just rolled, what a comical sight!

The onions all giggled, they just couldn't hold fair,
As the spinach kept spinning in some leafy despair.
A tomato wore shades, looking suave and quite slick,
While the peas teamed up for a dance, what a trick!

The Alchemy of Growth

Digging my hole with a spoon and a fork,
Hoping for magic or maybe a stork.
I sprinkled some laughter, a pinch of delight,
And waited for wonders to sprout overnight.

The radishes plotted a silly parade,
While the broccoli grouched about sunlight this grade.
A cucumber slipped on a rogue patch of dirt,
And tumbled down laughing, oh, how it would hurt!

Nurtured Narratives

Every seed that I sow has a tale to explore,
Like beans that complain they are stuck at the door.
The zucchini recalls when it played in the sun,
While the parsley just giggles, "Come on, let's run!"

With each drop of rain, stories blossom and dance,
The garlic breaks down in a fit of romance.
A beetroot declares, with a flair and a swirl,
"I'm more than a veggie, I'm a root veggie girl!"

Harvested Hues

Out in the patch, colors flit all around,
The oranges sing high while the beets grumble down.
A corn stalk stands tall, with a hat made of silk,
While the peppers conspire, all drenched in sweet milk.

A harvest of laughter, a festival feast,
As the veggies perform, making joy never cease.
With every odd shape, with every bright cheer,
I take in the colors, and it's fun, never fear!

Seeds of Solace in Starlit Nights

Underneath the moon's big grin,
I tossed some joy, let laughter in.
Stars twinkled like my funny bones,
Each giggle grew, like garden loans.

Crickets played their night-time tune,
While fireflies danced, a bright cartoon.
My worries floated, light as air,
In this silly dream where none could dare.

Under the blanket of the night,
Even the owls joined in the flight.
With whispers soft, they shared their jest,
Nature's humor in a jestful quest.

I giggled at the moon's big face,
In the garden of whimsy, we've found our place.
With every chuckle, a flower sprung,
In starlit dreams, our hearts are young.

Nurtured by the Sun's Embrace

The sun woke up with a morning yawn,
Stretching out over the neighbor's lawn.
Its rays tickled daisies in delight,
While worms wiggled, sharing the light.

Chickens clucked their silly strut,
Bopping to the beat of the farmer's rut.
With a sunny grin, the garden grew,
Growing jokes like cucumbers do!

When tomatoes giggle in dolled-up red,
They whisper secrets to the dirt bed.
"Let's throw a party, let's have some fun!
Or maybe just chill, we're already spun!"

Bumblebees fluff out with a buzz,
Making honey from all the fuzz.
In the warmth of joy, we bask and play,
In this sunny world, we're here to stay.

Blooming Words in a Dappled Glade

In a secret spot where giggles bloom,
Rabbits hop over the mushrooms' plume.
Each word sprouted like a silly hat,
Wobbling about like a cheeky brat.

The leaves are laughing, green with glee,
As squirrels crack jokes that you can't see.
A waltz of whimsy, a tease from the breeze,
Nature knows how to tickle with ease.

Laughter blooms as the flowers rhyme,
With petals dancing, it's truly sublime.
Every bee buzzes a cheerful tune,
Swirling their wands like a dandy cartoon.

In a dappled glade, the fun won't cease,
Spreading sweet smiles like a fragrant piece.
So come join our giggle-producing parade,
In this joyful world, where laughter's made.

Tales of the Tenacious Twig

There once was a twig who dreamed so high,
Of tickling the clouds and painting the sky.
"Why can't I dance?" it wiggled with cheer,
With each little sway, it whispered, "I'm here!"

The wind, a partner, couldn't resist,
Whirled the twig in a swirling twist.
"Let's paint the town with colors so bright,
And cover the world in giggles tonight!"

Each leaf joined in, with a rustle and cheer,
Creating a symphony, playful and clear.
They laughed at the raindrops, as if they knew,
That life's little jokes make skies just as blue.

So the twig became a legend, you see,
With stories of joy carried far as can be.
A tale of a laugh that refused to sag,
In a world where giggles and joy never lag.

Sprigs of Serenity in the Heart

In a garden where giggles grow,
We toss our dreams like seeds in rows.
A rake chases worms with a silly grin,
While bees dance round like they're sipping gin.

Sunshine's laughter warms the light,
As daisies don boots for a silly flight.
With each sprout, we cheer and shout,
For every bloom, our joy's a rout!

A squirrel in shades gives a cheeky wink,
While daisies debate the best shade of pink.
Crickets make music, playing it loud,
We stomp our feet, we're part of the crowd!

Balloons of thoughts float high in the air,
As we share our snacks without a care.
To sow laughter's flowers, that's the plan,
With garden gnomes who are part of the clan.

The Fertile Ground of Thought

In the soil of ideas, we sow our dreams,
With shovel and laughter, or so it seems.
We dig up puns while planting the roots,
And laugh with the worms in our funny boots.

A sprout of a joke peeks out of the earth,
And we water it well with giggles of mirth.
Thoughts bloom like flowers in vibrant hues,
As butterflies debate what path they'll choose.

Potatoes are pondering their fate with flair,
While carrots are practicing their stand-up air.
Lettuce shivers in laughter, it's quite the scene,
In this garden of chuckles, where fun reigns supreme.

Sown Silently, Harvested in Time

A silence so loud when the seeds we toss,
The veggies are gossiping, "Is that a loss?"
Tomatoes tiptoe and carrots prance,
While zucchinis love to wiggle and dance!

Nothing says humor like watering cans,
Performing their ballet with laughable plans.
In the quietest soil, secrets take root,
And sprouts of success start wearing a suit.

In harvest we gather our giggliest finds,
Radishes making the wildest of signs.
We cook up a feast of puns and delight,
In this kitchen of laughter, we dine every night.

The Symphony of Sprouting Senses

A concert of sprouts begins with a cheer,
As we lean in closer, the laughter's near.
The orchestra's tuning, with carrots on strings,
And beans do a jig with the joy that it brings.

Let's sing with the daisies, let's hum with the thyme,
As we tickle the leaves to a jazzy rhyme.
The peppers throw a spicy soirée,
While radishes roll in the comedy ballet.

Each snicker a note, in this green serenade,
Lettuce performs as a cool charade.
With sprigs of delight, we dance all around,
In a garden of laughter, our joy is profound.

Voices of the Verdant

In the garden, I slipped on the grass,
A worm winked at me, a mischievous sass.
A tomato danced wildly, an unripe green,
While carrots held court, a vegetable scene.

The daisies all giggled, swayed with delight,
As I tripped on my rake, in broad daylight.
The sunflowers chuckled, their heads held high,
"Why plant seeds for poems? Just watch us fly!"

The cucumber's a jester, gives everyone glee,
Sprinklers chase butterflies, what a sight to see!
In this merry patch, the weeds were astute,
Standing tall in a row, claiming their loot.

So come join the fun, hear the plants tell a joke,
While the beans all conspire beneath the oak,
Laughter grows louder, in this leafy brigade,
Where every fruit whispers, "Hey, we've got it made!"

Corners of the Coral

Beneath the waves, where the seaweed sways,
A crab read a book on the sunniest days.
Clownfish wore ties, quite dapper, you see,
While starfish threw parties, as bold as can be.

Anemones blushed, caught in the fray,
Bubble-blowers giggled at fish gone astray.
"Let's have a dance!" cried a shrimp in delight,
As jellyfish floated, all glowing, so bright.

Seahorses twirled, with style and a grin,
While octopuses juggled, and pulled the fish in.
Corals held meetings, dressed up for a chat,
Sharing seaweed snacks, a real diplomatic spat.

So swim on, dear friends, in this lively parade,
Where laughter and friendship will never be frayed.
In corners so coral, with mischief and cheer,
The ocean's a stage for all creatures sincere!

The Balance of Blooms

Roses wore hats, all fancy and proud,
While daisies played poker, cheering out loud.
Lilies sang ballads, a frequent refrain,
While bees buzzed along, just high on the gain.

Sunflowers debated the best kind of light,
Begonias snickered, "Don't you look bright!"
The tulips, in pairs, danced a waltzing jig,
While violets chuckled, "Let's dig, dig, dig!"

Pansies were plotting a grand costume play,
"Who needs a garden? Let's throw it today!"
With petals a-flutter and leaves full of sass,
The whole patch erupted, "Let's party en masse!"

So bloom, little flowers, with flair and with zest,
For nature's a stage, and you're all at your best.
In balance and laughter, our colors unite,
A garden of giggles, what a joyful sight!

Verses in the Verdancy

In the meadow, the grass took a bow,
As the daisies composed a song right now.
A squirrel in a top hat played piano in style,
While the mushrooms did pirouettes, all the while.

A butterfly ballet, oh what a scene,
It joined with the flowers, so vivid and green.
"Let's write some verses!" the breeze whispered low,
As the poppies made patterns in a marvelous show.

The oak tree recited a tale from the past,
Of raindrops and sunshine, how long they would last.
With laughter erupting, the ferns shook their fronds,
While a herd of wild daisies danced in the ponds.

So gather around in this playful expanse,
Where each bloom's a word, and we're all in the dance.
Nature's own library, a whimsical spree,
In verses of verdancy, joyous and free!

Dew-Drenched Dreams at Dawn

Morning breaks with a giggle,
Dew drops bounce like a wiggle.
Flowers yawn and stretch so wide,
Sunshine loves a joyful ride.

Squirrels gossip in the trees,
Whispering tales with the breeze.
Bees in tutu's start to twirl,
Nectar dances, watch it swirl.

Worms throw parties underneath,
Soft and squishy with their sheath.
A snail slides in with grace so grand,
"Slow and steady wins the land!"

Laughter sprouts up all around,
Nature's joy is truly found.
With each giggle and each sprout,
The world smiles, leaving doubt out.

Tending to the Roots of Reflection

Digging deep with a shovel wide,
Down below where the critters hide.
A mouse holds court with a wise old toad,
Discussing life on the winding road.

Roots like fingers spread out wide,
Tickling thoughts as they coincide.
They whisper secrets soft and low,
"Life's funny, didn't you know?"

Chickens in capes roam the ground,
Pecking answers, wisdom found.
"Cluck if you dare!" they all exclaim,
In the garden, it's all a game.

With every root, a chuckle grows,
Silly thoughts sprout, as everyone knows.
Reflection bounces, joy takes flight,
Sunset laughs, and stars ignite.

The Dance of Leaves and Letters

Leaves do a waltz in the breeze,
Whirling round with grace and ease.
Letters twirl like playful sprites,
Falling down in funny flights.

A cat with boots joins the show,
Bounding 'round like an old pro.
Each leaf whispers its own tale,
Of dancing squirrels and a mighty snail.

A paper airplane sails on high,
Chasing dreams that kiss the sky.
With every flap, giggles soar,
Nature's laughter forever more.

As twilight dims, the stage stays bright,
Leaves and letters in wild flight.
In this dance, each word will gleam,
A funny and whimsical dream.

Whimsy Among the Wildflowers

Wildflowers bloom with silly faces,
Tickling bees in their flowery places.
Petals dance and sway with glee,
Inviting all to join the spree.

A butterfly dons a bright top hat,
As ladybugs cheer, "What of that?"
They spin and twirl under the sun,
In this garden, all is fun.

Bees with bandanas buzz a tune,
While ants march in a silly swoon.
Their tiny feet tap out a beat,
Making flowers sway, oh so sweet.

With every color, laughter springs,
Whimsy lives in the joy it brings.
In wildflowers, where spirits rise,
Nature giggles under the skies.

Radiance of the Written World

In a garden where words grow,
Laughter sprouts, and thoughts flow.
Puns and rhymes dance in the sun,
The sillier the better, oh what fun!

With a shovel made of quirk,
Digging jokes, like hidden perks.
In this plot, humor does bloom,
Tickling minds, dispelling gloom.

Watch metaphors blossom bright,
Giggles sprout with pure delight.
Each line a seed, wild and free,
In this comic garden, come see!

Sow the seeds of wit and cheer,
Harvest laughter, bring it near.
With every joke, a new sprout grows,
In this realm where funny flows!

Wildflowers in the Ink

Ink spills forth like a wild vine,
Coloring verses, oh how they shine!
Each stroke a petal, tickling the air,
Wildflowers giggle, without a care.

A daisy's pun, a sunflower's jest,
In this bouquet, they're all the best.
Witty weeds weave through the prose,
Blossoming smiles wherever it goes.

The quirkier the joke, the thicker the stems,
Blossoms of laughter in rhyming hems.
In every line, a chuckle awaits,
Mirthful blooms, let's celebrate!

Grabbing joy from the garden's heart,
With every stanza, a funny part.
No thorns here, just giggles and grins,
Wildflowers of humor, where joy begins!

Cultured in Contemplation

In a library lush with thoughts,
Books sip tea while tying knots.
Verbs in monocles, nouns in a tie,
Wordplay dancing, oh my, oh my!

They ponder puns with playful glee,
Where each joke is a fine pedigree.
Pages flutter in laughter's breeze,
Chortles echo, bringing ease.

With a pinch of sarcasm, a dash of jest,
This literary feast is simply the best.
Debating drollery in each little nook,
Oh, what a joy, all from a book!

As metaphors sip their cafe lattes,
Witty baristas serving every say.
In this cultured land of wit's grand tale,
Humor thrives, and laughter prevails!

The Sprouting Verse

In the soil of silly thoughts,
Nurtured by jokes that laughter brought.
Every line a sprout to grow,
Tickles of fun, in rows they show.

With a trowel made of quick-witted tea,
Digging deep for hilarity.
Each pun planted with tender care,
Watch 'em bloom in the joyful air!

Chortling cliques in rhymes do play,
Sprouting chuckles in every way.
From verse to verse, the humor flows,
A garden of giggles, how it glows!

So let's sow seeds of laughter loud,
In this quirky, funny crowd.
Watch the sprouting verse take flight,
In whimsical ways, it feels so right!

The Meadow's Tale

In a field where daisies prance,
A carrot dreams of a silly dance.
The beans compete in a fluffy race,
While lettuce hides with a blushing face.

The sun sets low, a golden hue,
A pumpkin sings a tune or two.
The bugs all cheer, a lively crowd,
As flowers sway, both tall and proud.

A squirrel juggles acorns with glee,
While butterflies sip on sweetened tea.
The meadow's chatter, a joyful noise,
Where nature's chuckles weave the joys.

Even the weeds feel quite grand,
With a secret garden party so planned.
Laughter echoes in every nook,
In this lively, leaf-filled storybook.

Inflorescence of Thoughts

A daisy's got a joke to share,
About a tulip in need of air.
The radish winks with a cheeky grin,
While pondering where the fun begins.

Green peas whisper their clever schemes,
Of how to win in sunshine dreams.
A cabbage, wearing a clever hat,
Notes where all the laughter's at.

Sunflowers spin tales tall and wide,
About the bees who dance with pride.
Nature's humor, a delightful spree,
In the garden of giggles, can't you see?

Fruits and veggies, all in a row,
Chuckle together as breezes blow.
With every sprout, a jest unfurls,
In this patch of laughter, life twirls.

Whispers of the Wild

The forest rustles with playful vibes,
Where vine and twig tell goofy jibes.
A squirrel chuckles at the moon's bright glare,
While feathery friends enjoy the air.

Mushrooms giggle with polka dots,
As laughter echoes in friendly plots.
The oak tree whispers wise old tales,
Of mischief brewed in gusty gales.

The wildflowers dance in jaunty rows,
With petals that tease as the soft wind blows.
Each blade of grass shares a fleeting joke,
As gentle breezes weave the yoke.

In the wild's embrace, humor grows high,
With each tiny ant that waves goodbye.
In every shadow and bright ray,
Laughter blooms in nature's play.

Volumes in the Vegetable Patch

In the patch where cabbages sprout tall,
Tomatoes plot—the great vegetable ball!
Zucchini riffs on a jazzy tune,
While carrots dance under the bright moon.

Peppers boast how they're spicier still,
With radishes daring for a thrill.
The beets tell tales, all rosy and sweet,
In a garden filled with laughter, life's treat.

Each veggie speaks with a quirky flair,
They share stories that pepper the air.
Lettuce rolls with mirth on the floor,
In this cozy green literary core.

With every harvest, a new tale grows,
As laughter weaves through garden rows.
A patch of joy, concealing its craft,
In volumes of giggles and garden draft.

Inked in Green

With a pen dipped in spinach, I scrawl,
Hydrangeas and haikus on the wall.
Rhyme and thyme, a garden planned,
With verses sprouting from my hand.

Each stanza a weed, I'll let them grow,
Giggles and giggles, they put on a show.
A sunflower giggles, a rose cracks a smile,
Nature's own punchline, all the while.

I tickle the tulips with playful prose,
Chasing monsoons, till the laughter flows.
Bumblebees buzzing to the beat,
Nature's chorus, oh so sweet!

So let your ink dance with delight,
In every petal, find your light.
With every word, a sprout we find,
In this garden of laughter, we're intertwined.

The Poetry of Growth Motivated

In the garden of words, let's dig a bit,
We'll grow up rhymes, never quit.
Sprouting verses, wild and free,
Insects chime in, 'Are we the bees?'

A cucumber's joke, not too reaping,
Makes the carrots laugh while they're sleeping.
Tomatoes while blushing, get all the praise,
As we scribble our sonnets through the haze.

Worms in the soil, writing their script,
On decomposed dreams, they took a trip.
With quips and quarks, life's sprouts emerge,
Creating a comedy, a giggling surge.

So grab your trowel, the mulch of wit,
With each little seed, don't dare to quit.
In soil of rhymes, laughter will bloom,
From funny lines, we puff out the gloom.

The Orchard of Expression

In an orchard where laughter grows,
Fruits of humor, as everyone knows.
Apples of puns hang blissfully round,
While oranges joke with a zesty sound.

Plums in the shade spin tales of delight,
While cherries unite for a fruity night.
Each fruit a punchline, ripe for the pick,
Tasting the laughter, it's laughter's trick!

Under the branches, shadows do play,
Where words sprout up like weeds in a fray.
Bananas slip with a grin so wide,
In this silly orchard, I take a ride.

So swing by the trees of giggles and glee,
Harvest the joy, bring your spirit to see.
For in this delight, our hearts do reside,
In the orchard of words where fun is our guide.

Roots of Reflection

In the garden of thought, I dig deep,
Where memories sprout and giggles creep.
I found a trowel, all rusty and old,
Much better than silver, or so I'm told.

Worms dance and wiggle, oh what a sight,
They're critiquing my poems, with sheer delight.
I write them a sonnet, they twist and twirl,
Saying, "Keep going, you silly old girl!"

The sun shines bright on my silly face,
While squirrels discuss my poetic grace.
They chatter away in a bush nearby,
I hope they don't steal my words for a pie!

With roots that stretch far, and dreams that grow,
These quirks and oddities put on a show.
I plant my verses, just wait and see,
A funny old journey, it's just me!

The Blooming Page

On a page of paper, my verses sprout,
Each line a petal, don't you doubt.
The ink is the soil where they take flight,
Bumbling and tumbling, oh what a sight!

A bee buzzed by, said, "What's that buzz?"
"Just my latest poem, oh give it a whuzz!"
The flowers all laughed, in colors so bright,
"You've got the rhythm, now let's take flight!"

A butterfly landed, with a wink and a grin,
"Just for your words, I'll flap and spin!"
I waved my pen, it flitted away,
What a fine friend found on this funny day!

With laughter in bloom and joy all around,
Each word is a seed that's joyfully bound.
So come join the fun, don't be afraid,
Together we'll dance on this blooming page!

Beads of Dew on Letters

I spilled my ink like morning dew,
Turning pages into a water zoo.
The letters all giggled, said, "Look at me!"
"I'm glistening bright like a bumblebee!"

Puddles of nonsense forming with glee,
They trickle and splash, just wait and see.
With beads of laughter, oh what a play,
Each drop a story, come join the fray!

I found a snail, slower than thought,
"A poet?" he mused, "You surely have caught!"
I told him my tales, as he wriggled along,
He chimed in with rhymes, soft and strong.

So, here's to the weird, the wacky, the fine,
Where letters take shape, and all intertwine.
With dew-drops of joy on the stories we tell,
Let's splash in the puddles, and giggle as well!

Rhizomes of Rhyme

Beneath the surface, rhymes intertwine,
Roots bursting forth, oh aren't we divine?
A cacophony of giggles, in tunnels we crawl,
These hush-hush whispers, will thrill one and all.

Each word is a sprout, waiting its turn,
To pop from the earth, and watch the sun burn.
The soil is rich with laughter and cheer,
As critters convene, they all gather near.

I pulled up a pun, oh what a surprise,
The earthworms all chortled, rolling their eyes.
"You tickle us pink! You're a real delight,
Keep rhyming your way through the day and night!"

In this underground party, we twist and we twine,
The rhizomes of rhyme, in freedom we shine.
So let's dance with the roots, let's not be shy,
In this garden of giggles, we'll reach for the sky!

Sprouts of Imagination

In a garden of giggles, weeds dance and prance,
The carrots wear pants, oh what a romance!
Tomatoes play hide-and-seek with their mates,
While radishes joke of their round little fates.

The cucumber's silly, does yoga with flair,
While lettuce debates if it's too green to care.
Peas laugh in pods, a merry troupe's jest,
In this plot of humor, they're truly the best.

Sunflowers wear sunglasses, basking in light,
With daisies that giggle all day and all night.
The bees join the fun, in a buzz and a hum,
In this patch of delight, who said life's so glum?

So sow your own laughter, let mischief take seed,
In this row of hilarity, laughter's the need!
Grab a trowel for fun, dig deep with a grin,
In the soil of imagination, let the laughter begin!

Roots that Reach for Sky

Have you seen the radishes, roots stuck in a chat?
While up top, a carrot wears a stylish hat!
They dig in deep, but dream of the air,
Like veggies with wings, swirling everywhere.

The beets pulling pranks, they hide and they seek,
While carrots just blush, feeling silly and meek.
The onions are crying from laughing so hard,
As the broccoli flexes like a leafy bard.

Roots dancing wildly, a crazy conga line,
While the chives lead the way with a whistle divine.
They twist and they twirl, oh what a grand show,
Tangled in laughter, let the good times flow!

So let's dig together, break ground with a cheer,
For roots that reach high, let's give them a sneer.
In the garden of giggles, let's all take a chance,
And grow our own roots in a joyful dance!

Petals of Hope in the Breeze

Fluttering petals, in colors so bright,
Dancing in circles, oh what a delight!
A daisy with spectacles shares tales from the past,
While roses gossip, their whispers so fast.

The marigolds chuckle, with faces so bold,
As tulips tell stories of fortunes untold.
The wind carries laughter, like seeds in the air,
With every soft giggle, a story to share.

Petals flap wildly, like flags in a race,
In this garden of humor, there's never a trace
Of sorrows or worries, just joy on the breeze,
As flowers unite in a chorus of tease!

So let's twirl with the blossoms, let laughter take flight,
In the fields of our fancies, everything feels right.
With petals of hope, together we'll sway,
And find that life's best when we join in the play!

Cultivating Dreams in Quiet Gardens

In a plot full of whispers, dreams sprout with ease,
As tomatoes tell secrets, the squash shares its cheese.
The peppers, they chuckle, with spicy delight,
While beans stretch their limbs, reaching new heights.

In the shade of the cabbage, they plot and they scheme,
With radishes grinning, the rulers of dream.
The chard sings a tune, oh isn't it grand?
As the broccoli juggles some dirt in its hand.

Together they wander, in thoughts that go far,
Imagining places where veggies are stars.
With garlic as comic relief in the air,
While the peas gather laughter, as only they dare.

So come join this garden, where whimsy takes flight,
Cultivating joy in the soft moonlight.
In quiet, sweet laughter, let dreams bloom and grow,
In this cultivated space, we'll joyously sow!

Harvesting Words

In a garden of letters, I sow my quirk,
Nurturing puns with a shovel and smirk.
Pulling out verses like carrots from dirt,
Each word a veggie, sometimes a dessert.

Gardening tools made of ink and a pen,
Planting my humor, I laugh 'til I bend.
A weed in the rhyme? Just a silly thought,
Pull it with laughter, and the joke's never caught.

Sunshine and moonlight, my biggest delight,
Weeding out worries, everything feels right.
Fertilizing giggles with each silly phrase,
Harvesting joy on my wordy maze.

So come grab a shovel, let's dig in the fun,
Rhyme after rhyme, we're never done.
Each quip and each pun is a bloom that we've sown,
In this garden of laughter, we've truly grown.

Inked Blossoms

With inked petals dancing on vibrant pages,
Sprouting up humor like grapes through the ages.
Words blossom brightly in this quirky land,
Where metaphors giggle and playful trees stand.

Dandelion dreams take flight in the breeze,
Whispering jokes that come with such ease.
Growing a garden of laughter anew,
Rooted in sunshine, watered with dew.

We prune the dull phrases, let blossoms unveil,
Each sentence a flower, each giggle a trail.
Fragrant with whimsy, our thoughts in full bloom,
Bright colors of laughter, they'll banish the gloom.

So join me in scribbling these inked delights,
Where humor takes flight in fantastical heights.
With every stroke of the pen, we create,
A garden of giggles that's never too late.

Serenity in the Seedbed

Among the seedbeds where silliness grows,
I sprinkle my humor, let laughter compose.
Each line a tiny sprout, playful and spry,
   Tickling the funny bone, oh me, oh my!

The chill of the morning, a joke in the air,
Soft petals of punchlines flop everywhere.
We water the quips with some giggle-filled rain,
   And watch as they bloom without any strain.

With every sunrise, new laughter's in view,
A patchwork of whimsy, all fresh and like dew.
In this peaceful garden, where silliness thrives,
   We gather the chuckles, the joy that revives.

So come, my friends, to this tranquil space,
Where fun takes root and humor finds grace.
Together we'll grow, let our giggles expand,
   In the seedbed of joy, hand in hand!

The Rooted Muse

In the soil of my mind, ideas take flight,
Rooted in nonsense, they grow day and night.
A whimsical muse, with a wink and a grin,
Taps on my shoulder and says, 'Let's begin!'

I dig with my thoughts and plant them with flair,
Each line a wild flower, a joke beyond compare.
With laughter as sunlight and rhymes as my rake,
I'm gardening giggles—what fun can I make?

So come pull some weeds; let's clear out the ho-hum,
Making way for the chuckles, the joy, and the fun.
In this patch of pure nonsense, we frolic and play,
Harvesting smiles at the end of our day.

With roots intertwined, in this funny pursuit,
We grow a wild forest where laughter's the fruit.
So gather around, let's share what we choose,
For in this green haven, we celebrate muse!

Fostering Flourishment

In a garden of laughter, we scatter joy,
With spades made of giggles, not a toy.
Watering cans spill secrets bright,
As we dance with the daisies, oh what a sight!

We toss in some puns with each little seed,
And watch as they sprout, fulfilling our need.
Who knew that a smile could grow so wide?
In the soil of our humor, we take great pride!

Each weed that pops up is a joke we embrace,
With sunflowers grinning, we pick up the pace.
A tidbit of mischief, a sprinkle of cheer,
And soon our whole garden gives laughter a cheer!

So let's gather our friends for a fertilizers' feast,
With veggies and puns, we'll never have least.
The harvest of giggles is the best of all,
In this funny little garden, we'll stand proud and tall!

The Art of Cultivation

With trowels of laughter, we dig in the dirt,
To plant cracks and jests, oh how we'll flirt!
The beans may grow tall, but the jokes grow high,
As humor takes root, touching the sky!

We'll weed out the frowns with a chuckle so light,
And sprinkle our hopes with confetti delight.
A cabbage of comedy, a lettuce of fun,
In this whimsical plot, we all become one.

Each day brings a giggle wrapped up in the sun,
As we nurture our dreams, our work's never done.
And if things should wilt, we just plant them anew,
With a splash of bright laughter and a pinch of 'Woo-hoo!'

So grab your garden gloves, let's tend to the cheer,
In the art of good humor, there's nothing to fear.
From saplings to smiles, we cultivate glee,
Joining hands in the soil, oh what a jubilee!

Midday Sun on Daffodils

Beneath the bright rays, daffodils dance,
In the warm afternoon, they take a chance.
With hats made of petals, they sway left and right,
As butterflies chuckle at the silliness in sight.

A picnic of puns near the flower bed blooms,
With giggles popping up, the joy just resumes.
These sunny-faced blooms beam from their stand,
As we share goofy tales, right on the land.

Midday madness wraps us in bright sunny hues,
While bees buzz in rhythm, humming our tunes.
The daisies all whisper, 'Come join in the fun!'
For every bright flower knows laughter is spun!

With smiles all around, we toast to the day,
A concoction of fun that just won't decay.
As laughter and blooms fill the bright open space,
We frolic with flowers—a playful embrace!

Fertile Imagination

In the plot of our minds, ideas take root,
Sprouting silly thoughts, oh what a hoot!
With seeds of whimsy buried down deep,
We harvest our dreams while we giggle and leap.

Fertile imaginations burst forth with glee,
As we coax out the laughter, come join us, you'll see.
With tools made of whimsy and shovels of jest,
We cultivate joy, we're truly blessed!

Each corner we tend is a fantasy land,
Where unicorns prance, and funny things stand.
A sprinkle of nonsense, a dash of delight,
In our garden of humor, the world feels just right.

So let's sow our ideas and watch them take flight,
With imagination's magic, we'll twinkle so bright.
In fields of laughter, we all can partake,
A bountiful harvest of joy we will make!

Blossoming Stanzas

In a garden of giggles, we sow our dreams,
With puns that sprout, bursting at the seams.
Witty weeds tickle, as laughter takes flight,
Watch our words wiggle, in the moon's soft light.

Jokes bloom like daisies, brightening the plot,
A chorus of chuckles, we harvest a lot.
Silly phrases grow, like beans in a stew,
A comedy garden, where smiles sprout anew.

Roots of the rhymes tangle under our feet,
While echoes of laughter make our hearts beat.
In this wacky wonder, we dance and we play,
Each stanza a petal, floating away.

So gather your humor, let the fun unwind,
In this orchard of laughter, the silly you'll find.
Our verses all frolic, with joyful decree,
Let's celebrate nonsense—come garden with me!

The Language of Leaves

Whispers of humor in the rustling trees,
Leaves share their puns carried by gentle breeze.
Branches bend low with a giggle and cheer,
Trunk holds the punchlines, jokes bright and clear.

Each leaf tells a story dressed in green hues,
Shaking with laughter, like they've heard the news.
Photosynthesis laughter in every vein,
Nature's own comedy, never in vain.

Bark has the wit that inspires a grin,
When twigs start to laugh, see where they've been!
So stretch out your branches, let humor ignite,
In the forest of fun, everything feels right.

The language of laughter, in foliage bright,
We speak in the rustles, under moonlight.
Let's gather our leaves, and share what we glean,
In the forest of funny, the best scenes are green!

Cultivating Creativity

In a plot full of giggles, we tend to our art,
With shovels of humor, we dig from the heart.
Each seed is a chuckle, each sprout is a pun,
We water them daily, then watch the fun run.

Trowels of laughter till the ground with great might,
Creating a canvas where silliness takes flight.
Our thoughts bloom like flowers with colors so bright,
Once pruned into prose, they take off in the night.

We weed out the worries, let joy grow instead,
In this garden of nonsense, we nourish our head.
With each little quirk sprouting fresh from the soil,
Cultivating creativity, our humor will toil.

So gather together, bring laughter in rows,
In these fields of delight, every moment just grows.
With smiles as our fertilizer, we flourish indeed,
Here's to planting our thoughts, to always succeed!

Blooming in Metaphor

Metaphors blossom in bright, sunny clumps,
Each line is a petal, with giggles and jumps.
We cultivate whimsy in verses so sweet,
Harvesting laughter, each phrase a treat.

With witty comparisons, our thoughts intertwine,
As roses of humor and rhymes so divine.
Figurative gardens where oddities play,
Sipping on nectar in a sappy ballet.

A sprinkle of nonsense to brighten the scene,
Chasing grey clouds with laughter so keen.
Watch similes sprout in a colorful dance,
In this field of delight, we all take a chance.

So come, join the chorus, let your heart sway,
In a world full of joy, we'll forever stay.
Blooming in metaphor, let's raise a cheer,
For the garden of giggles we hold ever dear!

A Garden of Lines

In verse we sow a playful rhyme,
Each syllable a tiny climb.
With humor sprouting, laughter flows,
Watch silly phrases as they grow.

The weeds of doubt we will outsmart,
With puns and quips, we'll play our part.
Digging deep with a shovel of glee,
In our wordy garden, come see me!

The blooms of laughter grace the page,
More vibrant than a circus stage.
With every line, a giggle bursts,
Our silly seeds, no need to thirst!

So plant your words without a care,
They're bound to sprout, just brush your hair.
A garden built on jest, take heed,
Just mind the ants, they love our seeds!

Budding Ideas

From little thoughts, we start to sprout,
With giggles mixed in every route.
Tiny seeds of humor we chuck,
In a soil of laughter and good luck.

The sun shines bright on cheeky dreams,
Growing tall like goofy beams.
With each line penned, our minds take flight,
Budding ideas, what a delight!

Grab your hat, let's cultivate cheer,
Through rhymes that tickle, never mere.
Dig those abs with laughter's tease,
Funny bones, let's plant with ease!

So gather 'round, all poets, come!
In this patch, we'll have such fun.
With every verse, new blooms we find,
A garden rich in joyful mind!

The Poetry of Growth

In the garden where rhymes embrace,
Funny lines find their own space.
Each quip a sprout, each joke a tree,
Growing wild and ever free.

We water thoughts with giggles bright,
In this realm of pure delight.
The compost of laughter smells so sweet,
With silly phrases, we can't be beat!

Watch as our word blooms break the ground,
With every chuckle, fun is found.
The sunlight beams on our silly prose,
In this poetic land where jester grows.

So come and sow your dreams with flair,
In this funny garden, there's room to spare.
With every line, our blooms will soar,
In the poetry of growth, let's laugh some more!

Sunlight on Fresh Pages

In the morning light, we scribble and play,
Words bouncing about in a bright array.
Ideas sprout from a chuckle or grin,
Each line a sunbeam where joy can begin.

As giggles dance on the fresh white sheets,
Every pun drips with sunshine treats.
The pages are warm, the laughter's contagious,
With each silly stanza downright outrageous!

Colors of humor burst forth with grace,
Funny lines jump and find their place.
In this garden of ink, we dance and sing,
With creativity blooming, oh what joy it brings!

So flip through the lines where the sunlight plays,
Let your heart giggle and your mind amaze.
On fresh pages, the fun never fades,
In this garden of laughter, good fun cascades!

The Language of Lilies Signed with Light

Lilies chuckle in the breeze,
Spreading secrets with such ease.
They tease the tulips, oh so bright,
Under the moon's soft, silver light.

Petals gossip, stems sway and dance,
In this garden of chance and romance.
Bees with their honeyed tales take flight,
Mixing laughter with pure delight.

Each blossom boasts a funny quirk,
Daisies smirk as they go to work.
Colors clash in a vibrant show,
Nature's jesters putting on a glow.

So come and join this leafy play,
Where giggles grow and worries stray.
In the patch where humor's rife,
Flowers bloom with a chuckling life.

A Tapestry of Tilled Thoughts

In a patch of soil, ideas sprout,
Thoughts in rows, no room for doubt.
Weave the yarn, and sow the cheer,
Creating dreams that bloom, oh dear!

Worms in jackets till and twist,
Planning feasts, but here's the twist:
They squirm with glee at pests' surprise,
Dancing under sunny skies.

We plant strange things like socks and hats,
Who knew gardens could host such chats?
Fungi giggle, tickling the ground,
While laughter echoes all around.

And in this plot, all's fair and bright,
Every seed a spark of light.
With every sprinkle and every smile,
We grow our joy just for a while.

Whispers of the Garden

Listen closely, hear the greens,
Whispers of the garden scenes.
Radishes poke their charming heads,
Making jokes from cozy beds.

Peppers blush and jest around,
Tickled by the playful sound.
Cucumbers crack wise in their space,
Rolling laughter, what a race!

Gardens filled with giggly glee,
Every sprout, a jester, see?
Squash wears shades, so cool and sly,
As butterflies flit and fly.

So come and hear the green-thumbed fun,
In this garden, we are one.
Where humor sprouts and laughter grows,
Among the plants, where joy bestows.

Sprouts of Imagination

Seeds of dreams in soil so warm,
Sprout ideas, take your form.
With quirky beans and winking peas,
Each one adds to the garden tease.

Imagine carrots dressed in style,
Strutting 'round with such a smile.
Radishes wearing tiny hats,
Debating over garden stats.

A gnome with jokes upon his shelf,
Gardeners laughing at themselves.
Nurturing sproutlings, wiggle and jig,
As kites in the sky do a silly gig.

Pluck the whims, don't let them fade,
Grow them bold in sunlight's blade.
In this whimsical patch we find,
Sprouts of fun to warm the mind.

Boughs of Inspiration Reaching High

In a forest of thought, I found a quirk,
Trees with mustaches, going to work!
Squirrels writing sonnets, oh what a sight,
Boughs of ideas, soaring in flight.

The owls are winking, with wisdom so neat,
While rabbits debate on who can't be beat.
Their giggles ring out, in a chorus so bright,
Nature's comedians, in the soft moonlight.

Pine needles whisper, with secrets to share,
A conifer giggles—"You call this my hair?"
With acorns as drums, they tap out a beat,
The night turns to jam, with rhythm, oh sweet.

Jokes sprout from the ground, with each little sprout,
"Knock, knock!" they cry, "Who's there?" "Trees, no doubt!"
A jolly parade, on a root-laced stage,
Where laughter is the seed, and joy is the wage.

Nature's Palette of Poetic Possibility

In a meadow of colors, I picked up a brush,
Daisies are giggling, they make quite the fuss.
Tulips in bow ties, painted wild and free,
Creating a canvas, just for you and me.

The sun, the grand artist, splashes yellow and gold,
While clouds tell tall tales, often silly, quite bold.
Butterflies flit by, in waltz and in swirl,
Turning each flower into a grand twirl.

A daffodil whispers, "Let's start a show!"
While sunflowers dance, "Just watch how we glow!"
With rhymes in the soil, we laugh and we play,
Nature's own workshop, where whimsy holds sway.

"Not just a weed, I'm a poet in disguise!"
Said a dandelion with twinkling green eyes.
In this garden of whims, every petal's a dream,
Where even the thorns join the laughter's sweet theme.

Harvesting Harmony in the Hidden Woods

In the woods where giggles grow wild in the air,
Twigs are strumming tunes, with nary a care.
Mushrooms are rapping, under cover of trees,
While the bushes do ballet in the gentle breeze.

The vines give high fives, as they reach for the sky,
While crickets hold concerts, oh my, oh my!
Each leaf tells a pun, in a rustling spree,
While hedgehogs tiptoe, sipping sweet tea.

The babbling brook giggles, with secrets untold,
"Did you hear the one about the tree so bold?"
It splashes and clinks, like a cheerful refrain,
With ripples of laughter that dance down the lane.

So let's gather our laughter, like berries in jars,
To savor the joy beneath twinkling stars.
Each chuckle a harvest, from roots deep inside,
In the hidden woods' laughter, we take our sweet ride.

The Garden of Verses Awaits

In the garden of rhymes, the flowers all jest,
Roses wear glasses, thinking they're best.
Sunflowers gossip, with petals so wide,
While tulips feel awkward, but laugh with pride.

A tomato recites, as bees hum along,
Their buzz is the chorus, to nature's sweet song.
Even the weeds join with style and with grace,
In this wacky garden, we all have a place.

The carrots are cracking each rooty old pun,
"Why did the beet blush? It saw the radish run!"
With laughter that sprouts, from earth's lively bed,
In this garden of joy, there's no room for dread.

So come take a stroll, and dance on the green,
With flowers and giggles, a sight to be seen.
Each verse is a bloom, each line is a seed,
In the garden of laughter, there's room for each need.

www.ingramcontent.com/pod-product-compliance
Lightning Source LLC
Chambersburg PA
CBHW072149200426
43209CB00051B/922